# JEFF BADU

# THE
# SUPER
# HUNGRY

## NINE ACTION STEPS TO TAKE
## HOLD OF INFINITE RESOURCES

*King & Justus*
BOOKS

Published by King & Justus Books, LLC
3030 NW Expressway Suite 200
Oklahoma City, OK 73112
**www.KingandJustusBooks.com**

Visit the author's website at **www.jeffbadu.com**

ISBN: 978-1-7349386-2-3 (Paperback)

Cover design by King & Justus Books

# DEDICATION

This book is dedicated to William Champion, the current Chief Operating Officer (COO) of Badu Tax Services, LLC. William is by far the hungriest person I know on the God-given earth. He always shows up no matter what and makes absolutely no excuses. William, you are truly a Champion. No matter the obstacles that come your way, you always find a way to overcome them and break through any barriers. I'm very thrilled to have you on my team, and I knew you were the right person to hand the keys to. I know that you will continue to maintain your hunger and drive. This will take you extremely far in your journey towards creating an abundant lifestyle, which you have demonstrated very well. Cheers to a bright future, champ!

# TABLE OF CONTENTS

# ABOUT THE AUTHOR

Jeff Badu is a parallel entrepreneur and a wealth multiplier. He's a Licensed Certified Public Accountant (CPA) and the Founder and CEO of Badu Enterprises, LLC, a multinational conglomerate that owns several key companies. His marquee company is Badu Tax Services, LLC, a CPA firm specializing in tax preparation, tax planning, and tax representation for individuals and businesses. Another key company is Badu Investments, LLC, a real estate investment company that acquires residential and commercial rental real estate properties in areas such as the South Side of Chicago in an effort to restore traditionally underserved areas. What sparked his interest in launching these companies is his passion for helping people minimize their tax liability and ultimately multiplying their money by investing it and building multi-generational wealth.

He's extremely passionate about financial literacy and currently hosts various financial literacy workshops throughout the country. In addition, he's a public speaker, and his overall mission in life is straightforward: to make a lasting positive impact in as many lives as possible, especially when it comes to their finances.

# Purpose Defined

My purpose in life is to inspire and support the super hungry to take hold of infinite resources to create an abundant lifestyle. Your purpose is who you are. I discovered my purpose in April of 2019 (with my beautiful wife, Yvonne Badu, sitting next to me), and it was delivered by the legendary Rick Justus and his wife, Monique Justus. This was arguably one of the best days of my life. It profoundly changed my life for the better. Everything has become much more meaningful in life, and I can wake up each and every day knowing who I am and do everything with a purpose. I feel refreshed and energized each morning, knowing who I am and why I do certain things. So why did I write this book? Because my purpose is to inspire and support the super hungry to take hold of infinite resources in order to create an abundant lifestyle. Welcome, my super-hungry warriors. If you're not super hungry, then please read no further.

# THE BIG NINE

$M$y, oh my. The super-hungry. When I think of someone who is super-hungry, I think of an individual who is so motivated internally that they can achieve anything on this planet that they set out to achieve. They're super-hungry. They are so motivated and inspired that they can go out and get it on their own. They don't need to be woken up. They wake up before their alarm. They don't need a reminder before a meeting. They send you an email beforehand letting you know how excited they are about the meeting.

They show up five minutes before the meeting, patiently waiting in the Zoom meeting room with their notepad. In comparison, others show up two to five minutes late expecting a handout and don't have their cameras turned on because they're just now getting out of bed (shameful, isn't it?). They even send you a thank you email right after the meeting before you get a chance to draft yours. They purchase your Infinite Wealth course before the content in the course is even released! Quite impressive.

Welcome, ladies and gentlemen, to "The Super Hungry - The Nine Action Steps to Take Hold of Infinite Resources." With that being said, let's talk about some of the items covered in this book. First, humble yourself with a sense of urgency. Second, know that anything is possible. Third, value learning with a super-hungry appetite. Fourth, access specific information from the right resources. Fifth, research your field in-depth, with a strategic focus. Sixth, expand your research in the right direction, infinitely. Seventh, master your craft with 10x more effort. Eighth, take full advantage of the abundant amount and ultimate resources available to you. Ninth, last but certainly not least, believe that you can tap into your God-given potential in a massive and impactful way.

Let's have a real conversation for a second. My purpose in life is to inspire and support the super-hungry to take hold of infinite resources to create an abundant lifestyle. One more time, for those who might have missed it. Please remember to be fully present and inspired with significance. Please pay very close attention and take notes as you may have read in my book "Infinite Expansion – How to Infinitely Expand Your Vision of Abundance." This is very important information, people. My purpose in life is to inspire and support the super-hungry to take hold of infinite resources in order to create an abundant lifestyle. Put on your seatbelt. We're about to go on a wild and adventurous ride.

# Chapter One

# HUMBLE YOURSELF WITH A SENSE OF URGENCY

∞

L et's talk about the first step. Humble yourself with a sense of urgency. Humble yourself. What does it mean to be humble? First, to be humble means that you're not overly aggressive, you're not abusive, and you're not full of yourself. You're basically someone who can say, "you know what, this has been given to me; I'm thankful, and I'm grateful for what's been given to me." I'm going to get on my knees and thank God for allowing me this beautiful gift. Let me humble myself so that I can create more out of what's been given me. Let me make lemonade out of lemons. Let me create a tax firm from the YouTube videos given to me. It doesn't boast excessively, nor does it have a big ego.

Humble to me means that you're grateful and thankful for what you have, and you're willing to go out and get more. Some people think the word humble means that you're just thankful for what you have, and that's it. That is a myth, in my opinion. You've got to go out and get more. You deserve more, and you can get more; we all can get more no matter what. Think about the abundant amount of resources that are on this planet. How can you limit yourself? Be thankful for what you have, but always strive for more. Take what's given to you and be happy for it, but don't stop there. The truly humble own up to the fact that they can and need to get more. It's not about being selfish here. We are simply striving for greater while always being thankful for what's been given to us. We are out to create an abundant lifestyle no matter what.

Humble yourself. Please ensure that you are not easily triggered by fame. Do not become arrogant just because you have a certain amount of money to the point where you believe that now you can stick your chest out or that you can belittle people. Don't look down on people. Be thankful for what you have, but never stop pushing for more. Help those who want to be helped. In my case, I help the super-hungry. I try to remain as humble and as humanly possible. I still wake up each and every day as if I have nothing next to my name. As if I've never accomplished anything in life before. Yes, I occasionally post accomplishments on social media for marketing purposes, but that is really only to motivate others to strive with me. Please remember that you can always get more if you want more. Now humble yourself with a sense of urgency.

Why is this so important as it relates to taking hold of infinite resources? Because once you realize that information (i.e., the resource) is available to you, then you can say, "you know what, I'm going to go out and get it today!" Not tomorrow. Not next week. Certainly, not next year, but today. Yes, today. Yes, we need to be patient at times, but you need to take action immediately when an opportunity arises! Why? This resource may not be available tomorrow. It might be taken away from you. They might take it and give it to someone else because clearly, you didn't want it bad enough. Don't rush. Act! Taking action is not rushing. You are simply acting with a sense of urgency as you should. If someone told you that you have a $1M with your name on it, but you have to take action within 24 hours and gave you the steps to claim the money, would you say, "I need to think about it?" You probably wouldn't, nor should you not take action. This is what I mean here. When you have an opportunity in front of you, take advantage immediately. Don't wait because if you do, it might not be yours today. Your time to shine is now! So go out and get it!

One day, we all have to go to the grave. We don't take anyone with us to our grave. We build our own legacy, meaning we have to do things that will make us proud. One way to build a great legacy is to take advantage of any and all opportunities presented to you. When you have a sense of urgency, that allows you to act quickly and react in a fast way. It's not rushed. Always remember the difference between acting quickly and acting rushed. When you act rushed, you tend to struggle. When you are rushed, you don't take a second to think through what you're doing. When you act quickly, you can take hold of all opportunities presented to you and allow nothing to get in your way of achieving greatness. You desire it, and quite frankly, you deserve it. When you act quickly, you take a second to think through the decision, and once you have a decent (not necessarily absolute) amount of confidence about the decision, then you make it! You have to take action. That's the point that I'm trying to make. If you don't take action, then someone else may seize your opportunity. Yes, it is yours! If you spend too much time making a decision, then you may not make it at all. Acting with a sense of urgency is using the right amount of time and at least committing time to think through the decision so that you understand the opportunity that's presented to you. Acting with a sense of urgency is essentially being presented with an opportunity, stopping any non-critical activities such as watching TV, embracing the opportunity, then taking some time to think through what's been presented to you. As long as the opportunity sounds good for you based on your gut, then go for it quickly! That's what I mean when I say act with a sense of urgency.

Don't wait until the world pauses to take action. Take action fast and take it now! If you see an ad on YouTube on how to start a business, you want to start and offers a FREE one-hour webinar, click the link and watch it. You rarely have anything to lose by watching the webinar. These are just a few examples of acting with a sense of urgency. If you sit around and wait, it may be gone. Also, please stop thinking everything is a scam. That scarcity mindset will trap you from achieving greatness. Instead, embrace the opportunities that are given to you. Remember, you're not necessarily rushing the process. You are simply saying to yourself, "Okay, I have the resource. I've done some due diligence on the credibility of this resource, and now that I've confirmed within myself that this is legitimate, let me go out and get it immediately."

Humble yourself with a sense of urgency. Let's get a bit deeper into the meaning of this. For me personally, growing up was a bit of a struggle. I came to the United States (U.S.) when I was eight years old, and ultimately, life was pretty tough. Things were very tough due to my environment and the people I chose to surround myself with. As a young child from Ghana, coming to the U.S. and getting acclimated to the American lifestyle was pretty tough for me. I did things that I had no business doing, and I simply took life for granted. I don't blame anyone but myself for this. I had choices, and I made the wrong ones. Life could've turned out much worse than it was had I pushed the limit even further. God was truly on my side and knew there was a way out.

With that being said, at the age of 16, my family and I took a trip/vacation back to Ghana. I had to humble myself because I saw struggle first-hand. For the first time in my life, I knew what it was like not to have much. I knew what it looked like for those who didn't have the opportunity to come to the U.S. I knew what struggle looked like, and I looked at it dead in its eyes. I knew what it felt like not to have basic resources in life, such as a bus to go to school. I saw a lady with not just one but two babies wrapped around her back. She was selling apples, oranges, bread, and whatever else it took to provide for those two babies. Can you imagine the back pain? Can you imagine the neck pain? Can you imagine how tired she was? What car? What daycare? What government programs? You see, out there (Ghana), you have to go out and get it. There are no handouts. Can you imagine witnessing this life with your own two eyes after taking life for granted for eight years?

When I saw that, I had to humble myself, and I said, "I need to go out and get these resources." I need to stop taking life for granted and stop throwing away opportunities. I need to be super-hungry at all times. If I don't make a change now, then life may get even worse. I need to go out and teach people about money and to be the pioneer behind financial and economic abundance for all of humanity. I had to act with a sense of urgency. That was truly the turning point in my life. Everything after that point, I did with at least 2x more effort. For me, it was either success or success. Failure was not an option. I had to tap into my faith and get closer to Christ, who I can do all things through. I needed to surround myself with like-minded people and mentors who were genuinely interested in my success. Life as I knew it has never been the same ever since, and I thank God for life-changing moments such as that Ghana trip.

Here's another example. A man, who at the time was homeless, was given a flyer by a stranger to attend a free real estate workshop. Most people in this scenario won't humble themselves to embrace the opportunity and make a decision to attend. Why? They think it's a scam. They say, "I don't have time for this. I don't have time for that." Well, what do you have time for then? The kids are at home. The kids need to be fed. I need to watch a movie. I need alone time. The dog ate my credit card? Seriously? These are merely excuses. If you want to do something in life, then you'll surely make time for it. They have a "let's think of every single excuse in the world not to have to attend this event" mentality.

To be honest, that's more ignorance. They don't even want to bother attending this workshop. They don't know who will be speaking (although it says it right there on the flyer). They don't know what they'll get out of it. Fear and ignorance keep them trapped in the scarcity mind-set, which does not allow them to excel further. They don't want to bother advancing their education by attending this FREE workshop.

Unlike many people in the world, the homeless man took hold of the resource that was given to him. He humbled himself. He said, "thank you, God, for what you have given to me." He said, "I need to go and attend this workshop." He took it upon himself to not make excuses, and he actually attended the workshop. He humbled himself and was thankful that he was handed the flyer. Now, the choice was to attend or not to attend. If he attends, great things can happen. If he doesn't attend, he goes back to his normal everyday life, and nothing happens. One is guaranteed failure. The other has a chance of success. The keyword here is "chance." By not taking action, he gives himself no chance. By taking action, he at least has a chance of success. He took a leap of faith, and he ultimately took the opportunity to attend the real estate workshop.

The man who invited him was so shocked to see the homeless man attend! The homeless man clearly had a sense of urgency because he attended the workshop that he was invited to. He didn't say, "oh, just let me know when the next one is." What if there is no next one? What if there is no tomorrow? What if the opportunity is given to someone else next time? You see, God has two paths for you. There's the path of good, and there's the path of bad. You get to choose the path. That's the beauty of life. You've got to have a sense of urgency.

Back to the story. The man who invited the homeless man said, "you know what, you are someone who took time out of your day to attend this real estate workshop. You didn't make any excuses. When I met you, you were homeless." I don't even know if you had any money, but as a test, I handed you the flyer to see if you would show up, and you did just that; show up." Wow! One of the keys to success in life is showing up. If you don't show up, you won't even know what's possible. He decided to show up, and next thing you know, the man who invited him mentored and coached him on different aspects of buying real estate. He taught him conceptual aspects of buying real estate, such as wholesaling, flipping, and rental properties. Then, he starts doing it himself. Who? What? How? The homeless man starts acquiring real estate by taking advantage of real estate government programs, and suddenly, he goes from being homeless to home full. He now owns over a million dollars worth of real estate. Talk about a legendary story. You've got to humble yourself with a sense of urgency if you're looking to take hold of infinite resources.

Another example. This one is extremely near and dear to my heart. There's someone who wanted to be on my team within our CPA firm, Badu Tax Services, LLC. When he found out that I had just started my own CPA/tax firm, this man took it upon himself to do some research on my firm and myself. He knew that we had an abundant amount of infinite resources available. You're talking about free education, free videos, and free blogs. If you go to my website right now, www.jeffbadu.com, you'll find an ample amount of resources. He said, "you know what, I'm grateful, Jeff. I'm so thankful that you have these resources for people." For me, part of being humble is having a sense of gratitude.

What did he do? He took hold of those resources with a sense of urgency! He said I want to join your firm and become a part of your success. He was very intentional and said that he wanted to join my firm today (at the time). He said, "I've heard enough. Where do I sign up? What do I need to do to take advantage of this opportunity? I don't have the time to wait. I am super-hungry!" An opportunity never even existed, to begin with, is the secret. We weren't actively looking for new team members at the time, but he knew that when there's a will, there's a way. He created something out of nothing based on his hunger, determination, and drive. He is someone who is super-hungry. He is someone who is so motivated as if there is no tomorrow. He says, "I'm living today as if there is no chance tomorrow. I have a sense of urgency, and I need it now. Jeff, if I walk away without a role in your firm right now, my family doesn't eat." He simply said, "I am ready. What can we do to make this work?" He wasn't begging; he was super-hungry!

He eventually became a team member and is currently performing very well. Humble yourself in a sense of urgency. The example I just gave you is the legendary William Champion, who is now the Chief Operating Officer (COO) of Badu Tax Services, LLC. This man reached out to me on Christmas Day in 2017 on Facebook and showed up at my office (home office) the next day. Talk about super-hungry! He drove all the way from the South Suburbs of Chicago and came to my office on time on the North Side of Chicago (over an hour drive). We were having a conversation on Facebook, and he literally drove all the way to my office and said, "Hey bro, I want to form a partnership with you. You guys have any opportunities available at Badu Tax Services? Here's my resume." He showed up without even knowing if there were opportunities available, to begin with. Now that's the true definition of super-hungry. This is why to this day, he is the hungriest man alive, in my opinion. Nobody on this planet had ever done that. Nobody. To drive to my office to see if I had opportunities available. Nowadays, you can barely get someone to get on the phone when you're presenting them an opportunity, and they knew of this opportunity before the call. That's what you call lazy and complacent.

This man saw an opportunity where an opportunity never existed, to begin with. He created the opportunity for himself and paved the way for others to later join the firm. I'm so thankful for this man. I love him like a brother. He saw an opportunity, and he humbled himself to understand that this was a potential partnership. This would take time to evolve because we weren't even a full year into the firm yet at that point. Being humble requires some patience as well. We weren't even in a year of operations, but he said, "I see an opportunity, I'm going to humble myself, and I'm going to act with a sense of urgency." For that, I will always respect him for being the champion and man that he is today. Humble yourself. Humble yourself! As a matter of fact, I want to dedicate this book to William Champion. My dedication is to the hungriest man of all time, William Champion. That's a prophecy that I spoke into existence as I was writing this part of the book. When you read the dedication section, you will notice that William Champion, the super-hungry warrior that he is, the champion that he is, is the one I dedicate this book to.

Understand and humble yourself with a sense of urgency because if you don't, then you will have problems throughout the journey. If you don't act urgently, then your opportunity may no longer be there for you. It may be taken away from you. Somebody else just might take it. It can be a job; it can be a business opportunity or anything in life. Take hold of that opportunity and humble yourself with a sense of urgency.

# Chapter Two

# KNOW THAT ANYTHING IS POSSIBLE

L et's talk about step two. Know that anything is possible. You can do anything that you set your mind to do. Anything that you set your mind to do is very well possible. Life is filled with so much potential. Life is filled with infinite and abundant opportunities. Anything on this God-given planet is possible. Let me give you an example. I have an uncle (whom I hope reads this book) that said to me, "you know what, you will never become a successful accountant. All accountants that are successful don't look like you. They're Caucasian. They're very intelligent (which I believe he didn't think that I was that intelligent at the time), and they're also very well connected." I humbled myself, sitting there shocked as I was listening to him. I was a young child when he told me this. I will never forget this day. I was maybe 16 years old at the time, and this was my blood uncle telling me that I couldn't become a successful accountant. Can you imagine your own blood telling you that you couldn't do something that you believe you were destined to do?

How does that make you feel? Would you cry? Would you give up? Would you say, "why me?" Would you commit suicide? What in the world would you do if your own blood told you that you couldn't do something? What did I do? First of all, at that point, I humbled myself with a sense of urgency. I said to myself, "you're wrong. I can do anything I set my mind to do. Just watch." Of course, talk is cheap. What specific action did I take? I started researching. I started talking to subject matter experts (accountants). I started seeking mentorship.

Why? Because I read a good book called the Bible, and it told me that anything on this planet that you put your mind to is possible. I can do all things through Christ, who strengthens me. I read half of the Bible when I was 16 years old, and I learned those principles. Anything is possible. Don't let anyone tell you anything different. I'm thankful today that we run a CPA firm that operates in all 50 states in the U.S. and over 25 countries. We have a growing client base, a growing team, and a growing firm. We are one of the most successful accounting firms on the planet. This is the opposite of what my uncle told me. My uncle told me that I couldn't become a successful accountant. My uncle told me that I couldn't be a successful CPA. How does that feel now, uncle? Do you still doubt me? I doubt he'll read this book. His scarcity mindset almost led me to another career path because apparently, I wasn't good enough for the career I'm in now. Let me humble myself and not go any further with this example. I pray that you never discourage someone from doing something they believe they are destined to do. Instead, motivate them to keep pushing and striving for greatness. You, too, can do anything through Christ who strengthens you. So can your friends and family. Always stay positive.

Understand that anything is possible. Anything is possible! Set your mind to it and do it. "Ain't nothing to it, but to do it", right? It's true. I mean, think about how fascinating the Internet is, for example. You can go there at any time and search for anything or anybody you want. Have you ever thought about how life came about? How can you just create something out of nothing? The Internet is something you can't even touch, and it's one of the most powerful tools on the planet. Think about the technology that was put into place behind the Internet. Think about how many times they failed but still created it. Think about how many people talked to the person who invented the Internet and said, "Hey, this is not possible; you can't do this around here; that will never happen." Get rid of naysayers in your life, by the way. They are bad business. I don't mean kill them (thou shall not kill). I simply mean distance yourself, humbly. Send them a text saying that you're going away for a while. I dare you. You know who these people are in your life. They will try their absolute best to hold you back. Some of these people are your own blood, like you know who.

Albert Einstein was one of the greatest philosophers of all time. He said it was possible to become one of the greatest philosophers of all time. His subconscious mind didn't allow him to think of anything different. Thomas Edison, who invented the light bulb, failed over 10,000 times. Over 10,000 times, and yet, he invited the light bulb. He didn't stop. He kept pushing because he knew that anything in life was possible. Understand that anything you put your mind to, you can do. Just put your mind to it and never forget your vision board. Always set your vision, what you truly want. Not what somebody else wants, but what you truly want. I really hope you read the book

Infinite Extension - How to Infinitely Expand Your Vision of Abundance in full. This is where I talk about the twelve steps to creating an abundant lifestyle. This is part two of the book where we're talking about, The Super Hungry - Nice Action Steps to Take Hold of Infinite Resources.

Never forget. Know that anything on this God-given planet is possible. Anything is possible! Let me tell you about a fellow named Noah, who was a character in the Bible. I tend to resonate with Noah very well. Essentially, God spoke to Noah and gave him a message. God said, "I'm about to destroy the world as you know it." Please take your family on this arch and get away from here. First of all, God put Noah to the test. Then, he put his people to the test. He said, "go ahead and let everybody know that the world is going to be destroyed and see how they react." They can leave with you on the ark and survive. If they stay on the planet as we know it, they will die. Those who don't listen and those who don't humble themselves with a sense of urgency will end up dying. What did Noah do? He, first of all, thanked God for this valuable information. As any man would do, he told his family first of the matter, packed their bags, then told everyone. No one listened to him except his family. Noah humbled himself with a sense of urgency and went on the arc with his family. The others? They ended up dying because it rained and poured so much that the face of the earth was wiped out. Yet, you see Noah and his family on the arc watching in shock. Noah is truly the obedient one. Noah acted with a sense of urgency, and he also knew that anything was possible by listening and being obedient. By putting his mind to something and being determined to get on that ark with his family, he was able to do it. He acted with a sense of urgency, and he was the only one with this family to survive when the world was recreated. I wish we had more Noah's in the world.

Understand that anything is possible, and be sure to take action when opportunities are presented to you. Kevin Garnett, a former NBA star on the Boston Celtics, won the NBA championship back in 2008 and screamed, "anything's possible!" very loudly. Yes, indeed, anything is possible. He didn't have any championships before then, and he finally won a championship with the Boston Celtics, which happens to be my favorite NBA team. They ended up winning the championship because they were all on the same page and understood that anything that you put your mind to is possible. They were truly a Championship team. Never forget that anything is possible!

# Chapter Three

# VALUE LEARNING WITH A SUPER-HUNGRY APPETITE

L et's talk about the third step. Value learning with a super-hungry appetite. Please keep in mind that we're not talking about formal education here. I believe it is important that you get a formal education. I don't see anything wrong with going to school to master your craft, but what we're talking about is pure learning. We're talking about you educating yourself and valuing it each and every day. You're like a lion in the cage, ready for food each day. If you don't eat, you don't sleep. You must be fed with education!

What does it mean to value something? It means to respect it, take action and actually go out and do it (i.e., learn). When I value something, I respect it, and I don't want to lose it. I will do anything in my power to keep it. If I lose, it will be devastating, and it most likely will be difficult to get it back. Although we hate using the word impossible, it may not come back to you because you don't deserve to have it anymore. Value learning and learn in a consistent, continuous process. You don't stop learning once you're done with school. I still spend over $50,000 a year in education and training, and I graduated from college with a Master's Degree in 2015. When you stop learning, you die.

Think about Warren Buffett for a second. He reads quite a bit throughout the day, and he's over 90 years old! He can easily retire, but he truly values learning and education. He knows that the day he stops learning is the day he dies. Therefore, he respects his books and never uses time as an excuse to not read. You see, he's one of the wealthiest men on the planet because he never stops learning. Other greats do the same if you study them very closely. When you stop learning, you die. Remember that.

You never stop learning. You should be learning something every single day. I challenge you to dedicate at least two hours to learning each day. I'm being very conservative here. I challenge you to take at least two hours each day to learn. Let's learn for just two hours every single day. That's it. Two hours. Commit 14 hours in a week to learning and see if that doesn't change the entire trajectory of your life.

I personally commit at a minimum, three hours to learning each day. Two hours toward personal development and one hour towards something relevant in my profession, such as a new tax law. As a CPA, you must commit to at least 120 hours of professional education/learning every three years. Me? I commit to 120 hours within 40 days. Do you see the difference? I commit to 3,285 hours every three years to learning, while my profession only requires 120 hours within that time frame. That means I'm 27x ahead in my education, and if you compound that with some interest, that's quite a bit of learning. I challenge you to treat learning as part of your daily routine. The average person watches three hours of TV each day. Why can't you commit two hours to learning? The answer? You can. You just have to commit to it and put your mind to it. Enjoy it. Do it!

They have a super-hungry appetite, meaning learn as much as you can. Now you want to be doing the right type of learning. Let's look at the right resources. I don't mean learn soap operas and read fiction books all day. That's not what I mean. When I say learn, I mean going out and actually learning something that you don't already know and truly value, or essentially, perfecting a new craft. You can also learn by brushing up on something you already know to test the waters and ensure you know your stuff. Value learning with a super-hungry appetite, meaning learn now and learn often. Learn now! Learn often! Be super-hungry for more education. That's the only way you can grow. The more you learn, the more you earn. The more you know, the more you can grow. When William Champion came to me, he understood that he had to learn. He knew who he was coming to. He had a super-hungry appetite for learning. He knew that if he didn't learn, then he didn't eat. I will always respect this man for that. He is super-hungry, like a lion in a cage ready to eat. Always value learning with a super-hungry appetite.

As William was learning all the time at the CPA firm, he became better. He became more efficient and more knowledgeable about taxes. The next thing you know, he starts teaching it to other people as well. What better way to master learning than to teach it to someone else? You must learn, practice, embody, and master to perfect your craft—shout out to Rick & Monique Justus. When you learn something and become so obsessed with it, you teach it to someone else. Value learning.

Thomas Edison tried over 10,000 times before inventing the light bulb. He was committed. He valued learning with a super-hungry appetite. Warren Buffett learns every single day. Most of his time is spent learning each day. He has a super-hungry appetite and is the greatest investor of all time. Why? He values learning. A lot of it. He doesn't know everything, but what he does know is that he doesn't know enough. What does he do? He learns, practices, embodies, and masters the companies he invests in—shout out to his mentor, Benjamin Graham, from whom he learned these principles. Next thing you know, he acquires companies below their intrinsic value at a bargain price. They go up in value, and he makes money. It's not always about the money, but his learning certainly paid off. That's how he became one of the wealthiest men on the planet and the greatest investor of all time. He is super-hungry when it comes to information. He's not one of those who says, "I'll just do it tomorrow; who cares about this information." He humbles himself, acts with a sense of urgency, and has a super-hungry appetite for learning.

You have to humble yourself and stay super-hungry. We've already gone over what super-hungry means, but let's review it one more time. To have a super-hungry appetite means that if you don't eat today, you will die. Someone who is merely hungry can wait a few hours or even a day to eat. Someone who is super-hungry? They need to eat now, or they literally die. They need to find the food now! They have to eat right now as we speak, meaning when you're learning, learn now. Learn now, and that's how you take hold of infinite resources. You see the resources, and you go ahead and take advantage of them now. Not tomorrow, but now. You see an article that is free and appears of value; go ahead and read it now. Don't wait another minute. What if the article gets deleted? What are you waiting for anyway? Why are you waiting? Are you waiting to get kicked out of school first to learn? Are you looking to lose your job first to learn? Or are you waiting for the world to end? What exactly are you waiting for? Value learning with a super-hungry appetite. Always learn. Learn now and learn often.

# CHAPTER FOUR:

# ACCESS SPECIFIC INFORMATION FROM THE RIGHT RESOURCES

L et's talk about the fourth step. Until this point, I've tested your mindset a bit to see where you are. Now let's get to the good stuff. Be sure to access specific information from the right resources. This is huge. This means that if you want to start a tax firm, you should probably research how to start a tax firm. Do your research on how to prepare tax returns or build a team of elite tax professionals. Join Facebook groups that have tax professionals in them and stay engaged. It's really simple.

Notice the right places that you should be. Trust your gut, for crying out loud. Your gut rarely fails you. When you go on Google, please be sure you're narrowing your search to information that is relevant. This means that if you want to start a law firm, don't look up how to start a mental therapist practice. Look up keywords that relate to law. Look up synonyms such as the word "attorney." If your industry says the best place to find resources is on the Internet, then what business do you have going out and reading the newspaper? If it says the Internet is the best place to do research, then do research on the Internet. 'Don't make this complicated, people. Follow your gut and what the sources say.

Now, you do want to be a bit flexible, and you want to be sure to give yourself options, but with the right resources. What's the right resource? It's one that you know is going to provide the right information. Access specific information. When we say something is specific, we mean that it's intentional and it's detailed. It's concrete and focused. It's laser-focused. Whether it's a tax firm, dental practice, law firm, bakery, whatever it is. Be sure it's specific research from the right resources. If you're looking to build wealth, put in your Google search "wealth building." Put in buzz words like "how to multiply wealth."

Here's a resource for you, www.jeffbadu.com. It's filled with an abundant amount of financial literacy resources, and most of them are free. That's right. Free of charge! You have no excuse now when it comes to searching in the right place for financial literacy resources. I have studied the greats such as Robert, Kiyosaki, Mr. Rich Dad Poor Dad and compiled these into easy-to-read/listen-to blogs, videos, and podcasts. If you want to build infinite wealth, you should probably check out the Infinite Wealth course, which can also be found on my website, www.jeffbadu. com.

Access specific information from the right resources. Be very specific in your searches. If you're looking to start a business, you should probably go to Google and research your industry. You should check out IBISWorld, where you can obtain industry reports. If you're looking to start a law practice or a law firm, you should talk to a lawyer who already has a successful law practice. You should probably go to networking meetings with lawyers and attorneys so that you can talk to them and maybe, get some insight into how they started their law practices. Maybe you should acquire a mentor. Someone who's in your field in order to get information on how to start the law practice or the business. It sounds so simple. It doesn't have to be complicated. Just go out there and do it! Trust me. Access it, meaning use your phone, computer, network, or whatever is currently available to you. Use family. It could be anything out there. Access specific information from the right resources. When I was looking to invest in real estate, guess what? I started joining real estate groups on Facebook and Meetup. I started attending real estate networking events, and I started researching real estate and how to build massive wealth through real estate. I found some key resources, such as Than Merrill, who taught me how to wholesale and flip properties.

I had to start somewhere. If you don't start, you will never get where you need to go to. I went on YouTube and Google. YouTube showed me videos about people investing in real estate. There were ads that popped up offering a free one-hour webinar, and I humbled myself with a super-hungry appetite and attended. What did I have to lose by attending something that I was interested in? I could've watched TV, but what good would that do for my real estate success and my journey towards building passive income? Use your time wisely. Time is your most precious asset on this planet. I heard on the radio about a free 3-day workshop. What did I do? I attended that 3-day workshop because I knew that it was a resource, and I needed it to get my real estate business going. It's so simple. When you find something, you do and act. You don't wait. Embrace it and take advantage of it. When? Right now! Go on Google and search for something that's relevant to what you want to do. You'll be surprised by what you find out. You've got to access specific information from the right resources. It's very simple. You've got to commit to it, and you've got to do it. Remember, "ain't nothing to it, but to do it." So do what Nike says and "just do it!"

# Chapter Five

# RESEARCH YOUR FIELD IN-DEPTH, WITH STRATEGIC FOCUS

L et's move to the fifth step. Research your field in-depth, with a strategic focus. Be strategic. There're two types of people in the world: tactical people and strategic people. If you look at almost all the people at the top in the world, you'll notice that they're very strategic. Jeff Bezos, Elon Musk, and Warren Buffett are a few examples. They're very strategy-oriented, not tactical-oriented. My advice is to be 80% strategic and 20% tactical throughout the day. I tend to use the 80/20 rule a lot, by the way. For example, if someone can do something 80% as good as you can, then delegate that task to that person. Eventually, they'll become 100% as good as you are, if not better. Another example is 80% of your revenue usually comes from 20% of your clients. So why not get rid of 80% of your clients to achieve more revenue? Sounds harsh right? Not quite. It's strategy.

Unfortunately, for most people in the world, they're the opposite. They're 20% strategic (if that) and 80% tactical. They focus so much on the nitty-gritty weeds of things that they don't take the time to really understand what it is they're doing. They don't strategically sit back and say, "you know what, this thing isn't working; we need to put our focus into this other thing that's working." They don't take time to research their field. They don't look at the IBISWorld report and say, "oh yeah, the tax industry is set to go virtual/online, so maybe, I should go online now as efficiently and as effectively as possible." By doing deep strategic thinking, think about how many more clients you can get by going virtual. Thank God for COVID-19 forcing people to go virtual, right? "Oh wow, the industry is going virtual. Maybe when I form my business plan (like we did back in 2010), let's go to virtual since that's where the industry is shifting."

Let's do taxes virtually is precisely what I said and did. I did my research, and that's what I discovered. I knew where the industry was going. And thanks to COVID-19, the industry was forced to go virtual. It's shocking how many tax/accounting firms are still doing things in person. Why? They haven't read the updated industry report. They're still stuck in their old ways and don't want to evolve, just like Blockbuster, who ended up bankrupt. Think about how many retail companies were wiped out like Sports Authority? Why? They simply didn't pay attention to the curve and were too stuck in their ways to evolve over time.

Most people are still behind. Some people had to leave my industry in 2020 when the COVID-19 pandemic was declared. Why? Because they didn't focus strategically. They were too tactical. They were too busy doing tax returns instead of spending some time looking at everything from a high level and making adjustments as needed. They did not have a strategic focus. They were more concerned about debits and credits, which is more on the tactical side. I chose to focus on the strategy. I said, "let me go out and build a team and not be a one-man soldier. How can you go to war with just one soldier? Let me go out and see how to bring on offshore/overseas staff." I heard about this offshore staffing when I was working at PwC. I was curious about this. Why in the world would PwC, one of the top four public accounting firms in the world, have staff overseas? They've got to be doing something right. I humbled myself and quickly did some research on this. I was shocked to find out how efficient and effective this method of hiring was. There are super-hungry and dedicated team members overseas that prepare tax returns accurately. They handle the nitty-gritty tactical data entry work, while my U.S. team handles the high-level review and strategic work. Makes sense, doesn't it?

Follow the trends. You mean to tell me that I can pay less money for team members to have work done more efficiently and, quite frankly, more effectively as well? Sign me up immediately! This is just one of many examples of why being strategic is so important. Strategically research your field in-depth. Try to explore your field as much as you can. Utilize the IBISWorld report. Utilize Google and do in-depth, consistent research in your field with a strategic focus. Be strategic, not tactical. The book "E-Myth Revisited" taught me about being more a strategic thinker. It taught me to be an entrepreneur as opposed to a technician. When you're too tactically focused, what happens is you'll be so into the weeds of things that you won't even take time to say, "Hey, you know what, let's take a step back and let's analyze some things. Let's see what's happening here vs. there, and let's see what we can do better."

When you're so tactical, you can't focus on these things because you're bogged down in the details. You're so into doing everything that you can't even take time to say, "you know what, this thing we're doing here; it's not right. We need to hire more qualified team members. We need to go offshore. We need a virtual assistant." What happens when you're doing something, and next thing you know, you've been doing it so long that you don't take the time to realize you've been doing the wrong thing this whole time? You end up in a rabbit hole, where you don't want to go.

Be very strategically focused. Often, I see way too many people being so tactical. They are far too tactical. Yes, they do the tax returns, but they're doing so much that they get burnt out. In 2018, I almost pulled the plug on my own firm because I was getting burnt out. I was too tactical. What happens when you're so tactical? You get burnt out, and you don't even enjoy the things you thought you enjoyed anymore. I actually enjoy doing taxes. Do I enjoy doing 1,000 tax returns myself? I don't because I would get burnt out. Thank God for Rick and Monique Justus bailing me out in 2018. I will forever thank them for this. You don't enjoy the things that burn you out. It's simple. Maybe 100 tax returns; I can handle that by myself. 1,000? No way. I need a team. I enjoy it partially because less is more. I'm spending more time on a few high-level returns that I understand, and now, I can strategically think through those returns to provide the best value to my clients. I can even teach my team even more about specific returns instead of trying to rush through it, and next thing you know, I make mistakes, the client is unhappy now, and now, we have a bad reputation in the firm. When you are burnt out, you rush. When you are burnt out, you make mistakes. You simply don't do a good job when you are under high stress. I teach this same concept to my team, by the way, to prevent them from burning out. You don't want your clients to leave you. You don't want that. What do we do to prevent this? We shift our focus from a tactical mindset to a strategic mindset. While we're doing our research, we are mastering our craft. We just want to ensure that we do it strategically, not tactically.

# CHAPTER SIX:

# EXPAND YOUR RESEARCH IN THE RIGHT DIRECTION, INFINITELY

L et's go on to the sixth step, which is to expand your research in the right direction, infinitely. What does this mean? I'm still doing research today in my tax field. I'm doing research on ever-evolving technology. What type of technology is in store for the future? What can we do to be most efficient, most accurate, and most effective on tax returns? How can we best add value to all our clients? I'm doing research today on technology that doesn't even exist yet. How? By starting somewhere and expanding on it. Why? I want to provide the best possible service to all our clients. I am committed to greatness. I have no room for subpar service. We must perform at our best at all times.

Expand your research and go in the direction that your industry is telling you to go. If your industry is telling you that people are going online, then be doing research around how to continue online and do it infinitely. Never stop doing research, or you will become stagnant and eventually go out of business. Infinitely means there's no end. There's no stopping point to something that's infinite. Consistently expand your research, no matter what. Now what I'm not saying is, "don't start." You should start somewhere. Sometimes, you have to learn by doing or by example. You have to learn from by practicing after you've learned the fundamentals. What I am saying is that as you have launched your business, keep expanding your research on that business.

You do not want to have analysis paralysis, where you don't make a move after having enough information to make an informed decision. You have to find the right balance here. Understand that you should learn each and every day. Expand your research in the right direction. If you're someone who prepares business tax returns, be sure you're expanding your knowledge on different line items on the business tax return. Maybe understand the strategies that can help clients obtain better tax deductions and lower their tax liability. Maybe expand your service offering from just tax preparation into tax planning, which we did from the jump. Maybe you're a lawyer, and you focus on real estate law. Or maybe you should expand your research on how to expand your revenue streams in real estate law to make money on the closings and how you can make money on some of the insurance policies that come with the closings.

Remember, it's not just about making more money, but it's also about doing the right thing. It's about helping people abundantly. It's about helping people move in the right direction. It's about living through your purpose in life. It's about impacting all of humanity or whatever your grand challenge is. Expand your research in the right direction, infinitely. Do it until the day you die. When you do die, be sure that you have someone in place to continue your legacy and your research. Researching is about finding ever-evolving solutions to problems you care about. You should not stop researching because when you do, that's when your mind dies.

# CHAPTER SEVEN:

# MASTER YOUR CRAFT WITH 10X MORE EFFORT

∞

O n to step seven. Congratulations for making it this far, by the way. Keep pushing until you get to the finish line and when you get to the finish line, create a new finish line after that. That's what we call the infinite mindset, ladies and gentlemen. There is no end to this stuff! Master your craft with 10x more effort. You are the master of your own craft. If you are a plumber, you know about the water system more than anybody else on the planet. If you're a tax accountant, you know more about taxes than anybody else on the planet. What does it mean to master something? To master something means that you're the best at that thing. Try to make it one thing, which means master one thing at a time. Don't be the jack of all trades. Master one thing, teach it to someone else, and then you can move on to bigger and better things. I mastered taxes before I mastered real estate. I mastered real estate before I mastered life insurance. Focus on one thing at a time, please.

Master your craft. Notice how it's your craft. Not anyone else's craft. It's yours! Master filing tax returns if you're a tax preparer. Master providing tax planning services if you're a tax consultant. Master the infinite resources that will allow you to create an abundant lifestyle. Master your craft with 10x more effort. What does 10x more effort mean? It means to push hard until you can't push anymore. To go hard means, you never let anyone stop you or get in your way. This means that you don't stop researching. Yes, you need sleep. Yes, you need to balance out your days. You should use the 8-8-8 rule, by the way. Eight hours of your day is dedicated to working (preferably strategic work). Another eight hours is dedicated to fun, leisure, learning, growth, and personal development. Last but certainly not least, the other eight hours are dedicated to sleep (I sleep more than anyone I know). Have that balance because it is extremely important.

However, master your craft when you're not sleeping. Learn as much as you can. How do you really master something? Teach it to somebody else. Experience is also one of the greatest teachers on this planet. You build a team, and you do it with 10x more effort. Building a team allows you to strategically put 10x more effort into the right things. It's crazy, isn't it? I don't mean 10x more tax returns by yourself. Put 10x more effort into doing more tax returns effectively and efficiently. One way to do that is to build a team and teach the skills you've mastered to someone else who can take the torch. You will be 10x more productive when you delegate the right tasks to the right people. The right task is one someone else wants to do. The right person is one who knows how to handle that task.

Always remember that you are the master of your craft. Don't let anybody ever outshine you on your craft. Make it a friendly competition with your peers. Let's say you're a photographer. Become the best photographer on the planet. Don't let anybody ever take better pictures than you. If you're a tax accountant, don't let anybody do tax returns better than you do. That doesn't always mean you have to be 100% accurate all the time, by the way. Better can mean better savings, better energy, and overall, better value. Master your craft. Be the best at what it is you do at all times. Never stop learning. That's how you become the best at what you do. Be the best at what you do.

Usain Bolt, who is a runner, is the best at what it is he does. He is the master of his craft of running. Every Olympics, you see Usain Bolt there, and this man can run faster than anybody I know. Why? He puts 10x more effort into running. He does everything harder than the next person. He goes hard! Going hard doesn't mean you don't get sleep. You should always be getting sleep, especially if you're in a field like I am, an accountant. What I am saying is he intentionally dedicates time to running and mastering his craft. You are the master of your craft. Don't let anyone tell you differently. Please be sure to put a price tag on your craft so that people pay for the value you have to offer to the world. Yes, you will do certain things for free at times, but please don't underestimate your value. Don't let anyone ever tell you anything different. You are the master of your craft. Own it!

# Chapter Eight

# TAKE FULL ADVANTAGE OF THE ABUNDANT AMOUNT AND ULTIMATE RESOURCES AVAILABLE TO YOU

O n to step number eight. Take full advantage of the abundant amount and ultimate resources available to you. This is huge. Take full advantage. This means that if you have resources there, then go out and get them and own them. Take advantage of them. Take hold of them. Grab them. Touch them. Read them. Write them. Look at them. Embrace them! There's an abundant amount of resources that are on this plant. God gave us all these resources for a reason, not just a season.

This is why it's important to act with a sense of urgency. Resources can be taken away from you if you don't take advantage of them.

For example, let's say there's a real estate program that allows you to buy up to a four-unit rental property with as little as 3.5% down payment (this is a real program by the way known as the Federal Housing Administration (FHA) loan. Let's say that you are looking into getting into the real estate business. Why in the world wouldn't you take advantage of this program? Because you think it's a scam? It's not popular enough? Cardi B doesn't have it all over her Instagram? Quit chasing the status quo. You should take advantage of that program. It will help you accelerate in your real estate venture and allow you to begin the journey of building a passive income.

Take full advantage of the abundant amount and ultimate resources available to you. Yes, you. We all have infinite resources available to us. Yes, some people have more resources than others, but we do, in fact, have infinite resources, nonetheless. You have to go out and find them. They are there. Trust me. When someone comes to you and says, I'm going to teach you about growing a business, and you want to become a business owner, you've got to take advantage of that with a sense of urgency. You've got to have a sense of urgency because if you don't, it might slip right through your fingers. What if that person says, "you know what, you didn't respond fast enough, and I want to go to the next person and teach him that craft of starting a successful business?" I see this happen all the time. I kid you not. You've got to take full advantage of your abundant amount and ultimate resources available to you.

When a book is given to you and deeply within (remember to always follow your gut), you believe that this book has shown you the opportunity to help you advance in life, then you have got to take advantage of it. Humble yourself and always respect what's given to you, but act with a sense of urgency. Act with a sense of urgency and read that book. Read it the same day and the next day until you finish it. Read it that same hour. What if it leaves your hands and goes on to the next super-hungry warrior?

Take full advantage of the abundant amount of resources. What does something that's in abundance mean? It means that there's so much of it that it's almost overwhelming. It means that you have more than enough of something. That's what it means to be abundant and to live in abundance. Take full advantage. Don't let anything get in your way of taking hold of this resource. To take hold is to grab. To take hold is to claim what's rightfully yours. If you don't, the next person will. As a matter of fact, I will. Just try me. If you give me resources, I will eat them up like a hungry lion because I know what it's like to not take full advantage of opportunities given to me before the age of 16. I took life for granted. I took my spiritual life for granted. I'm so glad I don't take it for granted anymore. I worship until I can't worship anymore. My spiritual life allows my spirit to feed the being within. Without my spirit, there's no body. There's nothing. I am nothing without my spirit. I can do all things through Christ who strengthens me.

I took full advantage of my spiritual life, and I used it to move me in the right direction. I used it to write this book. What you hear right now is not from me; you hear it from the spirit within. Please take full advantage of the abundant amount and ultimate resources available to you. Don't take life for granted. Don't take these infinite resources for granted because what's given to you can be taken away faster than they were given.

CHAPTER NINE:

# BELIEVE THAT YOU CAN TAP INTO YOUR GOD-GIVEN POTENTIAL IN A BIG, MASSIVE, AND IMPACTFUL WAY

∞

J ust like that, we're on to the last, but certainly, not least step. Keep pushing all the way through! You've got this. Believe that you can tap into your God-given potential in a big, massive, and impactful way. What does this mean? God has given you resources. God has given you opportunities. You've got to tap into your God-given potential. You're given arms, legs, eyes, a nose, abilities that no one else has, and vision. Tap into them in a big, massive, and impactful way. Don't let anyone outshine your gift. This is why you must keep perfecting it. Don't think of yourself as less than who you are. Don't boast. Be proud of who you are and consistently work on developing yourself. You have to be of value to yourself before you can be of value to others—shout out to Eugene Marshall.

Don't think of yourself as less than who you truly are. Think of yourself as more than who you are. Always tap into your God-given potential. Are you good at art? Then don't stop drawing. Go ahead and draw. Get a piece of paper out right now and draw! Keep drawing until you can't draw anymore. Find something that you're good at and keep doing just that. How do you find something that you're good at? First of all, you need to understand your purpose in life. What is your purpose? Who are you? What do you like to do? Research and learn the things you like to do. Start testing the waters a bit. See if you actually like it.

You can start shadowing people. You can acquire mentors who can guide you in the right direction. Tap into your God-given potential. Pray on your knees to God to help you find something that you love to do. Once you find it, never stop doing it! Only do it in bigger and better ways. You are the master of your craft, so you've got to take advantage of your God-given potential. You've got to tap into it. What does it mean to tap into something? It's to activate it. It's to be in the moment. It's to call it. It's to live in it. We have to think about the future, but we also have to live the moment. When you tap into your God-given potential, tap into it in a big way. How do artists become celebrities? They tap into their God-given potential and publicize their work to the world. They hire the right people to help promote their work. They go on tours. They conduct interviews. They use the right platforms to take them to the next level.

What does it mean for something to be a big way? It means that it's powerful. It means that it's impactful. It's massive. It goes beyond you and will live after you. Have a purpose so big and impactful that it genuinely means something to you. Have a vision so big that if the world were to see it, they would go blind. That's why my purpose in life is to inspire and support the super-hungry to take hold of infinite resources to create an abundant lifestyle. I help people create abundance in ways they never knew existed. I help people create passive income by acquiring rental properties and utilizing wealth-building methods that they never knew were possible.

I help people navigate through the three steps of creating infinite wealth. For more details on this, check out my Infinite Wealth course. I help people take hold of infinite resources to create an abundant lifestyle. Not a scarcity lifestyle, but an abundant lifestyle. That's a big thing in this world. Most people are scarcity-minded. I wanted to reverse that into abundance-minded. That's the God-given potential that's been given to me, and I'm thankful each and every day for God giving me this gift and allowing me to help others through him. Remember, I can do all things through Christ who strengthens me. I am a very spiritual person.

We all have a purpose. We just have to find it and live it each and every day. Don't ever lose who you are. Always understand who you are and what your God-given potential is. Find your purpose by going through a Purpose Day experience (shout out to Rick and Monique Justus for helping me find my purpose in life). Understand that we all have the potential to do something great on this planet. Find who you are and what you can do for people. Tap into your God-given potential in a big, massive, and impactful way, no matter what.

# PREVIOUSLY BY JEFF BADU

## Infinite Expansion

When it comes to life, everyone has a purpose. It doesn't matter what it is or what you do. The key is you have a purpose. Everyone on this planet has a profound purpose. It can be viewed as something that keeps you going. Purpose to me is the reason for your existence on this planet. It's about what can help and support people. It can be helping them with their finances. It can be a basketball player that allows people to empower their bodies or a fitness trainer who helps people create a workout plan that maintains a sustainable lifestyle. It could be a pastor who uplifts the church with his words. Everyone has their own profound purpose in life, and I would say that my real purpose is helping people take a resource that already exists in order to create an abundant lifestyle.

www.ingramcontent.com/pod-product-compliance
Lightning Source LLC
Chambersburg PA
CBHW050513210326
41521CB00011B/2445